Grandpa's Secret

Ruby U. Tunke

Copyright © 2012 by Ruby U. Tunke.

All rights reserved. No part of this book may be used or reproduced by any means, graphic, electronic, or mechanical, including photocopying, recording, taping or by any information storage retrieval system without the written permission of the publisher except in the case of brief quotations embodied in critical articles and reviews.

ISBN: 978-1-4525-5229-3 (sc)
ISBN: 978-1-4525-5228-6 (e)

Library of Congress Control Number: 2012908588

Balboa Press books may be ordered through booksellers or by contacting:

Balboa Press
A Division of Hay House
1663 Liberty Drive
Bloomington, IN 47403
www.balboapress.com
1-(877) 407-4847

Because of the dynamic nature of the Internet, any web addresses or links contained in this book may have changed since publication and may no longer be valid. The views expressed in this work are solely those of the author and do not necessarily reflect the views of the publisher, and the publisher hereby disclaims any responsibility for them.

Any people depicted in stock imagery provided by Thinkstock are models, and such images are being used for illustrative purposes only.
Certain stock imagery © Thinkstock.

Printed in the United States of America

Balboa Press rev. date: 05/21/12

I dedicate this book to all souls whether they be mature or newly arrived. Welcome and may you find an essence of home within these pages.

I am filled with gratituide for my partner Rob and my mother Elke. Thank you Rob for providing the space for me to Be Who I Am. Thank you Mom for your never ending support and belief in me. Lots of Love.

Brandy laid on her bed and allowed her mind to drift off onto all the events of the day. Events like riding her bike to school that day. She could still feel the warm breeze as it had flowed over her body and added to the joy she was feeling. The sound of her tires as they moved over the sidewalk and the sound of her grandpa's voice were still fresh in her mind.

Grandpa was chatting away about the beautiful day and how he had enjoyed days just like this one when he had been a young boy. Brandy loved to listen to the stories Grandpa told; stories about fishing and stories about his life. That is his life when he was still alive.

Some of the earliest memories Brandy had were memories of Grandpa. She felt very loved and special whenever she thought of him.

Today was a special day for Brandy. Today was the day Grandpa had promised to share a secret with her. Today was a day that Brandy knew would help her not miss Grandpa so much.

Grandpa had promised that today he would tell Brandy a secret so great that she would never forget how special she was. She was so special that she could have Grandpa with her whenever she wanted to.

You see, Brandy's Grandpa had died two years before and there had been a long time that Brandy was unable to feel Grandpa. Now Grandpa had told her that the knowing of this secret would mean that she would never again feel apart from him.

There was great excitement in the air as Grandpa started to speak. Sometimes Brandy heard Grandpa through her ears and sometimes she heard him as a thought that just popped into her head.

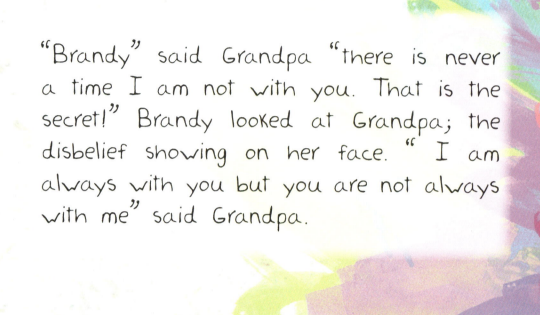

"Brandy" said Grandpa "there is never a time I am not with you. That is the secret!" Brandy looked at Grandpa; the disbelief showing on her face. " I am always with you but you are not always with me" said Grandpa.

Brandy looked at Grandpa and asked him to please tell her the secret again. "I am always with you but you are not always with me" he repeated.

Grandpa went on to explain "Your mind is filled with thoughts about your day Brandy and that makes your mind very full. I am energy that grows bigger when you think of me and I take up a lot of space in your mind. When your mind is busy with other thoughts it cannot make room for me. It is only when you quiet your mind that there is space for me Brandy. Because you control your mind all you have to do when you want to spend time with me is make room for me by letting go of your thoughts."

"Pretend your thoughts are like balloons. When you want to let go of balloons you just open your hand and release them to the sky. When you wish to let go of your thoughts all you have to do is imagine your mind opening and releasing your thoughts to the sky. This will create the most beautiful space for me. Some people call this meditation or prayer" said Grandpa.

Brandy made a funny face and thought about what Grandpa had just said. "Do you mean sometimes I am not able to sense you but you are still there and by meditating or praying I can talk with you anytime I want to" asked Brandy?

"That's right" said Grandpa. "I am always here but sometimes you are very busy with other thoughts and there may not be enough room in your mind for all your thoughts and me. Just meditate and know that I am there."

Brandy thought about this and knew it was true. She could talk with Grandpa anytime she wished to. A feeling of excitement sprang up in Brandy. It felt like a happy bubble that was inside her body and was getting bigger until there was nothing but the feeling of great joy.

Yes, this was a very special day and a most amazing secret. This was Grandpa's secret.

Maria Goncharova was born in Russia and raised in Turkey. She came to Canada in 2009 to get her Master of Design degree from the University of Alberta. Maria loves colourful things, tulips and can't live without her scarf collection. When Maria was a little girl, she enjoyed creating little books for her parents and friends.

CPSIA information can be obtained
at www.ICGtesting.com
Printed in the USA
LVIC091150170612
286387LV00002BB